T is for Trails
A Hiking Alphabet

Written by Judy Young and Illustrated by Sharisse Steber

PUBLISHED BY SLEEPING BEAR PRESS™

Trails to Travel

For each letter throughout *T is for Trails*, a family-friendly trail in a national park is described. It includes the state the trail is located in, the trail's round-trip length, and its difficulty rating. Difficulty ratings are not an exact science, and vary from source to source, but all are based on distance, terrain (land features), and elevation gain (uphill walking). A short trail may be assigned a *Difficult* rating because the elevation gain makes it really steep. A long trail may be rated *Easy* because it's relatively flat. Hikers vary, too: what seems easy to one beginning hiker may feel moderate or even difficult to another beginning hiker. Below is the rating system used in *T is for Trails*.

Easy–Wheelchair Accessible: A trail that is paved or has a hard surface. Its length can vary, but it is relatively level and has little to no elevation gain. These trails are for all ages and abilities.

Easy: A trail that is very visible or well marked. It is usually less than three miles and has only a slight elevation gain. These trails are for all levels of ability, including young children and those with no hiking experience.

Moderate: A trail that may or may not be as well marked or maintained. It is usually less than five miles long. It has more elevation gain, possibly with some steeper sections and uneven terrain. A little more challenging, these trails are for most people, including children and those with limited hiking experience.

Difficult: A trail that may not be well marked or maintained. It is usually more than five miles long, may have elevation gains with prolonged steep ascents and descents, and possibly some challenging terrain, such as rocky areas or stream crossings. These trails are for more experienced hikers, including older children.

Very Difficult: A trail that is usually not well marked or maintained. It can be any length. Often more remote and at high elevations, it covers difficult and hazardous terrain. These trails are for experienced and well-prepared hikers.

What Do These Mean?

Trail maps often use symbols that can be very helpful to hikers. A slash mark through a symbol means something is not allowed. Can you figure out what each symbol means?

Hit the trail and go for a hike! More than 57.8 million people in the United States hike, and hiking is Canada's most popular outdoor activity. No matter where you live, how old you are, or your level of hiking ability, there's a trail that's perfect for you.

Some trails are long, some short. Some are easy, some difficult. You may hike in rugged wilderness areas, going up and down mountains. Or your trail may lead you over flatter ground, taking you across rolling prairies, along the beach, or even over boardwalks. Often, towns and cities have trails at nature centers, beside rivers, down urban greenways, or through city parks. Some trails are paved, making it easier for families with young children, the elderly, or those differently abled to enjoy a hike in the great outdoors.

A Trail to Travel: Acadia National Park's Cadillac North Ridge Trail leads to the top of Cadillac Mountain, where you may be one of the first in the US to watch the sunrise. (Maine, 4.4 Miles, Moderate)

A a

A is for Ambling Adventures

Go for an afternoon's amble
down a footpath on a hike.
Awesome adventures on the trail
are for young and old alike!

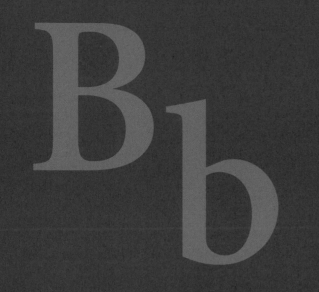

B is for Backpack

Take a backpack on your hike—
it's the perfect place to stow
all the things that you might need
to carry with you wherever you go.

Use a backpack to carry things you need or want on the trail. Kids as young as four can usually carry a backpack with their own snacks, water, headlamp, and whistle.

There are ten essential things someone in your hiking group should bring on every hike. They may never be needed, but if they are, you'll be glad you have them.

1. Water and food—more than you need
2. Headlamp or flashlight for each person
3. Whistle: each person should carry one
4. First aid kit—include insect repellent
5. Sun protection: sunscreen, sunglasses, and hat
6. Map and compass, and/or GPS device
7. Extra clothes—weather can change
8. Emergency shelter (poncho, space blanket)
9. Multipurpose tool or knife
10. Waterproof matches, lighter, or fire starter

A Trail to Travel: The Historic Blue Forest Trail in the Petrified Forest National Park wanders past blue-and-purple-striped hills and petrified wood. (Arizona, 2.4 Miles, Easy–Moderate)

There are shirts made with sun protection and moisture-wicking materials and pants that zip off into shorts. But if you don't have these, that's okay. Just wear the clothes you have.

Choose clothes appropriate for the weather, and wear layers—they can be put on or taken off if you get hot or cold. Even during hot weather, a long-sleeved shirt helps keep you from getting sunburn and insect bites.

Footwear? Keep in mind the terrain. If hiking a rocky, uneven trail, hiking boots with good traction and ankle support might be best. For less rugged trails, sneakers may be fine. Sandals and flip-flops are not a good choice—you don't want stubbed toes, sprained ankles, or dirt and rocks to slide in. Try to avoid cotton socks. They don't wick moisture as well as wool or polyester and may cause blisters.

A Trail to Travel: Carlsbad Caverns National Park lets you enjoy a unique underground hike past stalactites and stalagmites on the Big Room Trail. (New Mexico, 1.25 Miles, Easy–Mostly Wheelchair Accessible)

C is for Clothes

What clothes to wear is always a question.
Choose what's best for the weather.
A shirt? A jacket? And what about shoes?
Should they be canvas or leather?

D is for Distance

Go the distance; it's not that far—
  a mile or two to reach the end.
And while you hike, set smaller goals,
  like *I can make it to that next bend!*

Trails can range from less than a mile to thousands of miles long. However, a hike is a journey to enjoy, not a distance to cover. A common hiking phrase to remember is to "hike your own hike." That means choose how fast and how far you are comfortable going. If you're four to seven years old, you may be able to hike two to four miles. An eight- to twelve-year-old may cover five to eight miles.

It's okay to turn back before reaching the trail's end, but you can help yourself finish by making mini destinations, such as reaching that mossy rock or big tree. Then treat yourself to a mini reward, such as a handful of peanuts. Many trails have their own reward at the end—a beautiful view, a stunning waterfall, or an unusual rock formation.

A Trail to Travel: Denali, the tallest mountain in North America, looms above you with its snow-covered peaks as you hike the Gorge Creek Trail in Denali National Park. (Alaska, 2 Miles, Easy–Moderate)

E e

E is for Etiquette

Remember to use good etiquette—
be considerate, be polite.
Using trailside manners
makes everyone's hike a delight.

Everyone on the trail wants to have a good time. That's why it's important to use good trailside etiquette. So always use these good hiking manners:

- Be friendly and polite: say hello when you meet someone, thank you when someone lets you pass them.
- Be quiet: you can talk, but don't scream or shout. If you want to listen to music, wear earbuds.
- Don't hog the trail: walk single file if someone is coming in the opposite direction.
- Hikers going uphill have the right of way: step to the side if you meet someone while you're coming down a narrow trail.
- Let faster walkers pass you.
- Don't startle someone—let them know you are coming up behind them and passing them.
- At a pretty spot, take your pictures, then step aside to let others take photos.

A Trail to Travel: Emerald Lake Trail takes you to a glacier-fed jewel of a lake surrounded by jagged peaks high in Rocky Mountain National Park. (Colorado, 3.5 Miles, Moderate)

F is for Family Fun

When you hike on a trail together,
there's a lot of family fun.
Brothers and sisters, the baby, too—
hiking's for everyone.

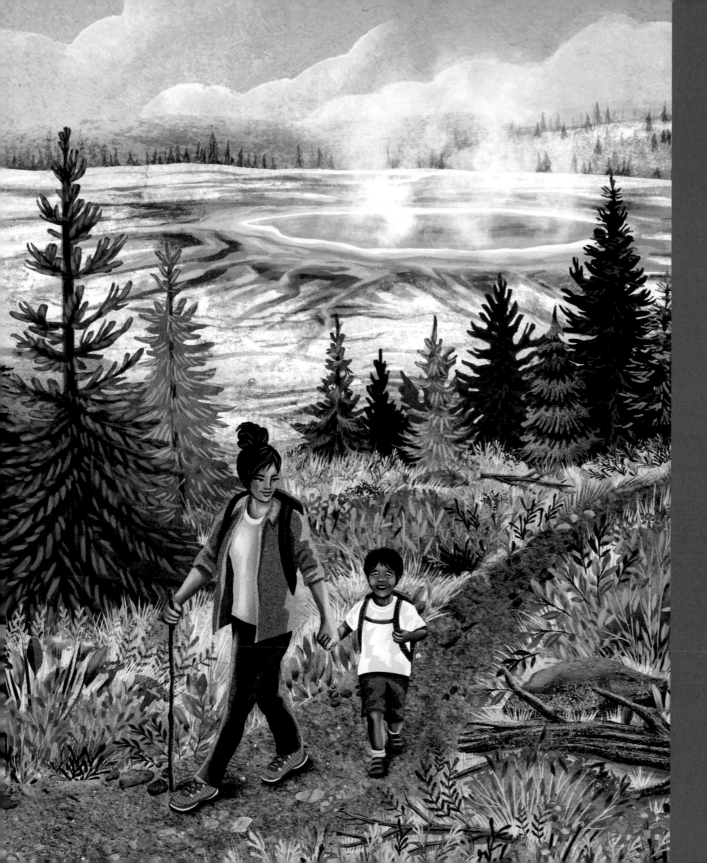

Hiking is a fun adventure for the whole family. Babies and toddlers can ride in child carrier backpacks. There are also backpacks to carry older children with special needs and trails that wheelchairs and strollers can go on.

Make the whole hike a family affair from start to finish. Kids can help choose their own snacks, fill their own water containers, and pack their own backpacks.

The whole family can choose which trail to explore. Do you want a trail with a stream to splash through or a lake to fish in? Maybe a trail with big rocks to climb on would be fun. Or perhaps one that leads to something awesome such as a natural bridge or where ancient petroglyphs are etched into sides of cliffs. Always remember, however, to follow area regulations about things like swimming, fishing, climbing, or touching.

A Trail to Travel: Fairy Falls Trail in Yellowstone National Park offers a beautiful waterfall, plus an amazing view of the colorful Grand Prismatic Spring. (Wyoming, 5.4 Miles, Easy)

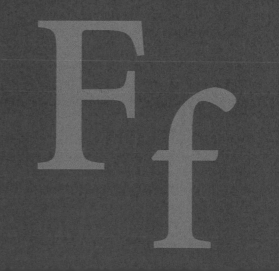

G is for GORP

Good Ole Raisins and Peanuts—
GORP's a tasty trailside treat.
It gives a boost of energy
that hikers love to eat.

In 1906, Horace Kephart, who helped create the Great Smoky Mountains National Park, said, "A handful each of shelled nuts and raisins, with a cake of sweet chocolate, will carry a man far on the trail . . ."

Almost every hiker has eaten GORP or some variation of trail mix. The raisins provide carbohydrates, which give quick energy, and the peanuts are packed with protein for more long-lasting fuel. Make your own trail mix by adding whatever you like: other kinds of nuts and dried fruit, M&M's, granola, sunflower seeds, coconut, sesame crackers . . . be creative!

When hiking, it's important to have plenty of snacks to keep up your energy. Some other healthy hiking snacks include peanut butter, beef jerky, tuna packs, veggie sticks, apples, and oranges. It's also nice to have some hard candies to suck on. They keep your mouth and throat moist, plus they give you an energy boost.

A Trail to Travel: The Georgian Bay and Marr Lake Trails present scenic views overlooking Lake Huron in Canada's Bruce Peninsula National Park. (Ontario, 4 Kilometers or 2.5 Miles, Moderate)

Gg

H h

H is for Hydration

Keep your body hydrated—
make sure you drink a lot.
Water is an important must
whether you're cold or hot!

Water is the most important thing to bring on a hike. If you don't stay hydrated, even on a chilly day, you could suffer serious health problems.

You should drink about half a liter per hour, more if it's hot outside. Drink regularly—a few swallows every 15 minutes keeps you hydrated better than chugging a lot at one time. Sports drinks help replenish minerals, but you should also drink just plain water. And don't forget to tank up before you hit the trail and after you get back.

Many hikers use water bottles, but water bladders held inside your backpack have a tube so you can easily sip as you walk. Don't drink from creeks or springs without using a water-filtering device. Even if the water looks clear, there are often invisible microbes that can make you sick.

A Trail to Travel: High Dune, with great views of the tallest dunes in North America, can be reached by picking your own path at the Great Sand Dunes National Park and Preserve. (Colorado, 2.5 Miles, Moderate–Difficult)

I i

Hiking is more than just walking—look around and explore. Are there animal tracks or scat (animal poop)? Do you see any food for animals? Have some fun with these exploration activities, too:

- Scavenger Hunt—before you hike, make a list of things to look for on the trail.
- Critter Count—how many kinds do you see?
- ABC Hike—find things that start with each letter (acorn, butterfly, creek . . .).
- I Spy—give clues for someone else to guess what you see.
- 20 Questions—ask yes/no questions to figure out what someone else sees.
- Take a magnifying glass—inspect bark, bugs, whatever you see!
- Look through binoculars—what's far away?
- Take a sketch break or do a leaf rubbing.

A Trail to Travel: Indiana Dunes National Park's Paul H. Douglas Trail winds through black oak savannahs where you may spy a butterfly on wild lupine flowers. (Indiana, 3.4 Miles, Easy–Moderate)

I is for Interesting Items

There are hundreds of interesting items
you might spy along the trail—
an odd-shaped rock, an animal track,
a flower, a nest, a snail.

It's fun to keep a journal of your hikes. Write down the date, trail name and location, distance, start/finish time, weather, and things that happened on the trail.

Journals are a way to go back and relive your hike another day. You'll remember if you saw a moose, and you'll certainly want to add that to your journal, but also write down some of the smaller details of your hike. Did you cross a stream on a split-log bridge? Was there still snow on high mountain peaks even though it was July? Draw a picture in your journal of something you saw or did on your hike.

A journal also helps you remember things you learn. Did you see wildflowers, butterflies, insects, or birds you didn't recognize? Look them up in an identification book or on a computer and write their names in your journal.

A Trail to Travel: Joshua Tree National Park is not only dotted with odd-looking prickly trees, but also with strangely shaped boulders like the one seen on Skull Rock Trail. (California, 1.7 Miles, Easy)

J j

J is for Journal

When you get home, grab your journal—
write where you went and what you saw.
And is there something special
that you might want to draw?

Joshua Tree
National Park

Desert
Tortoise

We hiked this morning and the ranger showed us some really cool reptiles!

Desert Spiny
Lizard

They change color to reflect the heat.

The sky is so dark here. I've never seen so many stars!

Big dipper

Some surprising words are used to describe the terrain (land features).

You're on a *knife-edge* when your trail goes along a narrow ridge with slanted drop-offs on both sides. If you hike over a *knob*, you go over a rounded hill, and if the knob has no trees on top, you're on a *bald*.

Your trail may have a steep *grade* to reach the summit (highest point of a mountain). But the grade may be flatter crossing a *saddle*, where the land dips between two higher points. A tall, skinny opening between cliffs is a *chimney*, a deep, narrow passageway is a *notch*, and a flat area with hills circled around it is a *basin*.

A small creek that joins another to make a bigger creek may be called a *fork*, and if you stand beside it, you're on the *bank*.

A Trail to Travel: Kīlauea Iki Trail takes you through a lava tube, across the basin of a volcano crater, and along the crater rim at Hawai'i Volcanoes National Park. (Hawai'i, 3.5 Miles, Moderate)

K is for Knife-Edge and Knob

Knife-edge, knob, fork, saddle, and bald;
please don't misunderstand!
These are words that are often used
when describing the land.

K k

L is for Leave No Trace

If you pack it in, then pack it out,
and follow the rule of Leave No Trace.
No one likes to see your trash—
everyone wants a beautiful place.

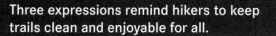

Three expressions remind hikers to keep trails clean and enjoyable for all.

Pack it in, pack it out. Don't litter—take ALL your trash with you to properly throw away later. Don't hide a wrapper under a rock or toss a banana skin into the woods. Fruit peels can take two years to decompose. Also, take out used toilet paper in a plastic bag.

Leave no trace—that you were ever there. Don't write on rocks, carve on trees, or make dams in creeks.

Take nothing but photographs, leave nothing but footprints. In many places, including national parks, it's illegal to take artifacts. If you spy an interesting rock or discover antlers or other natural objects, inspect and photograph them, but then leave them. This goes for flowers, too. Don't pick them—take a picture. Other hikers also want to enjoy them.

A Trail to Travel: Ledges Trail in Cuyahoga Valley National Park lets you scramble over boulders and explore nooks and crannies in massive rock walls. (Ohio, 2.3 Miles, Moderate)

A trail map shows you the path to follow. The map's *legend* explains what different symbols mean. It also shows that dotted, solid, or different colored lines represent trails, rivers, or roads. A *scale* tells distance, such as one inch equals a mile. The top of a map is always north, but the map may have a *compass rose* to show north, too.

Topographic maps have lots of wavy lines called *contour lines*, which show the shapes of hills and valleys. Numbers on the contour lines tell the *elevation*, or how high the land is along that line. The closer the contour lines are to each other, the steeper the land is. If the lines are almost touching, there could be a cliff, and if it makes a small circle, that's the top of a mountain.

A Trail to Travel: Mica View, Mesquite, Cholla, and Cactus Forest Trails make a loop through a spiky "forest" of saguaro, prickly pear, cholla, and barrel cacti in Saguaro National Park. (Arizona, 3.8 Miles, Easy–Partly Wheelchair Accessible)

M
m

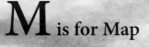
M is for Map

Take a look at a map:
    it shows where a trail will go.
First over a hill, then across a creek,
    up a mountain high to a valley low

N n

N is for National Park Service

It's easy to find a trail to hike
with spectacular sights to see.
The national parks have thousands of trails
that were made just for you and for me.

There are 63 US national parks, each filled with trails, but there are also trails at national monuments, national recreation areas, and national historical parks. There are also trails in national forests and grasslands, as well as in state parks. In Canada, hikers can wander along trails in 48 national parks as well as in provincial parks.

Try hiking on one of the eleven national scenic trails, such as the Appalachian Trail, which goes 2,190 miles from Georgia to Maine. You can hike a little of these long-distance trails as a day hike, backpack sections at a time, or thru-hike the whole trail from one end to the other.

With thousands of trails to choose from, there's a trail for you. And if you're new to hiking, many places offer ranger-led hikes.

A Trail to Travel: Notch Trail takes you into a canyon, up a ladder, and along a cliff with views of Badlands National Park. (South Dakota, 1.5 Miles, Moderate)

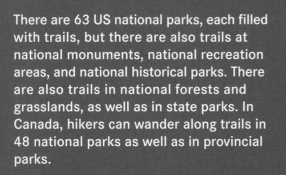

On an *out-and-back* trail, you hike one way, then turn around and come back on the same path. Don't worry that you're returning on a trail you've just hiked; trails look different when you go a different direction.

On a *loop* trail, you don't retrace your steps. The trail leads you on a big circle, starting and ending at the same place.

A *lollipop* trail combines an out-and-back and a loop trail. You go down the trail, make a loop at the end, then return the way you came.

A *point-to-point* hike starts and ends at two different places. You'll need a vehicle waiting or someone to pick you up at the end.

There are also *side* trails—trails that leave the main trail, often taking you to something interesting to see.

A Trail to Travel: Olympic National Park's Hall of Mosses and Spruce Nature Trails in the Hoh Rain Forest let you explore a moss-covered world with huge trees and ferns over-your-head high. (Washington, 2.2 Miles, Easy–Partly Wheelchair Accessible)

O is for Out-and-Back

Some trails go out
and then they come back.
But some make a loop
as you follow their track.

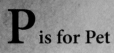

P is for Pet

Do you have a canine friend?
A pet that is your hiking buddy?
Watch out! He may jump in that puddle
and get his feet all wet and muddy!

Dogs make great hiking buddies, but remember to follow the B.A.R.K. rule!

Bag your dog's waste.
And pack it out with you!
Always leash your pet.
Loose dogs can get lost or come upon dangerous hazards like cliffs or fast-moving water. A leashed dog lets other hikers feel safe and comfortable, too.
Respect wildlife.
Dogs can hurt wildlife and wildlife can hurt dogs—another reason to use a leash.
Know where you can go.
On some trails, dogs are not allowed, so check before you go.

In addition to B.A.R.K, remember that your dog needs water; bring plenty for both you and your dog, and a collapsible water bowl, too.

A Trail to Travel: Parker Ridge Trail ends looking down at the Saskatchewan Glacier, the largest in the Columbia Icefield of Canada's Banff National Park. (Alberta, 5 Kilometers or 3.1 Miles, Moderate)

Enjoy the peace and quiet of a trail. If you are noisy, not only might you disturb other hikers, you won't be able to hear the sounds of nature.

Is the wind whispering through the trees? Did you notice how that hawk's screech echoed through the canyon? What about insect sounds? They click, snap, buzz, and whine. A twig just snapped. Shhhh! Is a deer walking nearby?

As you hike, notice smells, too. Does that wildflower have a scent? Can you smell pine trees? Dry leaves? A waterfall?

What do things feel like? Is moss wet? How cold is the creek water? Is the canyon's slickrock rough or smooth? Be careful, though; you don't want to touch poisonous plants or get stuck by a cactus.

A Trail to Travel: Queen's Garden and Navajo Combination Loop at Bryce Canyon National Park will take you past hoodoo rock formations. (Utah, 2.9 Miles, Moderate)

Q q

Q is for Quiet

When you're out on the trail, be quiet and listen.
What are those sounds you hear?
A trickle of water, a rustle of leaves,
the buzz of a bee or the step of a deer.

R r

R is for Rules

When you hike, follow the rules,
 and safety is rule number one!
Pay attention and use your head;
 play it smart and your hike will be fun.

Follow these rules to stay safe when you hike:

- Don't hike alone.
- Stay within sight and/or voice range of an adult in your hiking group.
- Be careful—rocks can be wobbly, roots can trip you, and even leaves can be slippery.
- Respect wildlife—don't get close.
- Don't eat wild berries, plants, or mushrooms unless okayed by an adult.
- Learn to recognize dangerous plants, such as poison ivy or stinging nettles, and don't touch them.
- Before you hike, tell someone where you're going and when you expect to be back.
- Be prepared with your 10 essential items.
- Don't assume you can rely on cell phone access if there is a problem.

A Trail to Travel: Rock Harbor Trail in Isle Royale National Park leads to Suzy's Cave and a four-thousand-year-old inland sea arch formed by Lake Superior's waves. (Michigan, 3.8 Miles, Moderate)

TRAIL RULES

- NO LITTERING
- HIKE WITH A FRIEND
- STAY ON TRAIL
- NO DOGS
- RESPECT WILDLIFE

Know what to do if you get lost.

When you hike, each person should always have their own whistle. The ONLY time you blow it is if you are lost.

If you get lost, STOP and STAY. Don't keep walking. Don't try to find your way back to the trail. Sit down and try to stay calm. Blow your whistle three short bursts. (If you don't have a whistle, yell "help.") Then listen. If you don't hear a response, blow it three more times, and listen again. Your hiking group will be looking for you, so do that over and over.

If you have a phone and can get a signal, call someone you know for help. If no one answers, call 911. There are trained rescue people who will find you.

A Trail to Travel: Schoolhouse Gap Trail is colored with spring wildflowers or fall foliage as it rambles through the Great Smoky Mountains National Park. (Tennessee, 3.8 Miles, Easy)

S
s

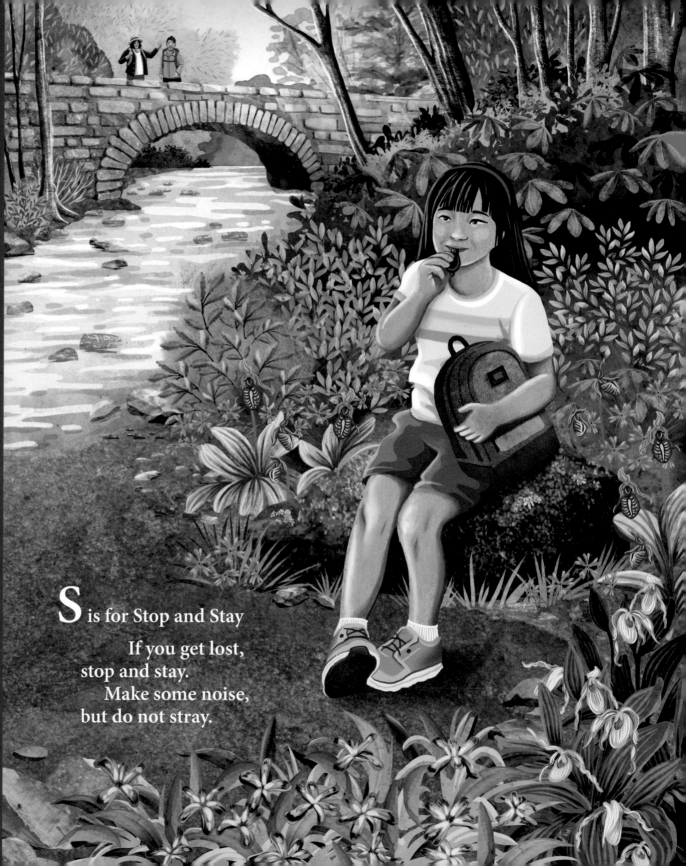

S is for Stop and Stay

If you get lost,
stop and stay.
Make some noise,
but do not stray.

Tt

A *trailhead* is the start of a trail. It usually has a *trail sign* that names the trail and may also tell how long it is or how far to an interesting spot.

A *trail marker* shows your path. Sometimes the marker is a *blaze*—a vertical rectangle painted on a tree. The number of blazes and their positions on the tree tell if the trail is turning. If two trails cross, each will have a different color blaze. Some trails are marked with metal or plastic tags nailed to trees; some are marked with posts.

Cairns—rocks stacked on top of each other—often mark trails that don't have trees. When you reach a cairn, look for the next one and walk toward it. Don't knock down or make your own cairns; doing so may confuse other hikers and they could get lost.

A Trail to Travel: Twin Creeks Trail in the Great Smoky Mountains National Park has you splashing across creeks on a warm summer day. (Tennessee, 4.5 Miles, Easy–Moderate)

TWIN CREEKS TRAIL

T is for Trailhead and Trail Markers

Trailheads, *trail markers*, and *trail signs*
　　are terms hikers use when they talk.
Cairns and *tags* and *blazes* on trees
　　will show the direction to walk.

U is for Urban Hiking

Go urban hiking on a city trail
when you can't get out of town.
Find a greenway or a river walk
that your feet can take you down.

It's not always possible to get out to a wilderness trail, but don't let that stop you from hiking. Urban hiking—hiking in a city or town—is a great way to explore not only nature but also your community.

Many cities have trails. Some are scenic river walks. Others may weave through greenways, which are strips of land that wind through developed areas. Urban trails may also be located at nature centers, in city parks, or at historic landmarks.

The same safety rules apply to urban hiking as to a hike in the wilderness. Plan where you're going to hike, making sure it is a safe place. Don't go alone. Wear proper walking footwear, dress for the weather, and take water and snacks. Also, make sure you follow all traffic rules, such as using crosswalks and obeying traffic lights.

A Trail to Travel: Use the Jefferson National Expansion Memorial Trail to wander around the Gateway Arch National Park, the only national park set totally within an urban area. (Missouri, 1.8 Miles, Easy–Wheelchair Accessible)

Hiking trails don't make themselves and they don't take care of themselves, either. Trail building and maintenance is often done by volunteers.

On National Trails Day—the first Saturday every June—many hiking and trail clubs have volunteer days where you may clear trails, pick up trash, or help with other projects. But don't do any projects on your own without permission from the agency responsible for the trail's maintenance. Logs you may think need to be moved may be left that way on purpose to correct or prevent erosion. Brush piles may be left to provide shelter for animals.

There are also "adopt-a-trail" programs. Volunteers agree to hike a section of a trail several times a year, keep it clean, and report things like fallen trees or broken trail signs.

A Trail to Travel: Virginia Falls Trail in Glacier National Park not only gives you a blast of misty air-conditioning at the end, it also takes you past the thunderous roar of St. Mary's Falls. (Montana, 3.2 Miles, Easy)

V is for Volunteers

Here's to all the trail volunteers—
to them a great big thanks is due!
They take their shovels, picks, and rakes
and work to keep trails nice for you.

Spotting wildlife is always exciting when you take a hike.

If your trail goes through a *riparian* zone—an ecosystem where land meets moving water such as a spring, creek, or river—you're in prime wildlife habitat!

Many animals hang out near water. You may catch sight of a heron, spot all sorts of songbirds, or even spy an owl. Did you see that bright blue dragonfly, glimpse that salamander darting under a rock, or notice the row of turtles sunbathing on a log? An otter, muskrat, mink, or beaver may swim by. A raccoon or fox may come to take a sip. Deer or moose may be grazing on the lush green vegetation.

Trails can take you through all types of ecosystems. You may observe an alligator floating in a cypress swamp, detect a Gila monster in a desert ecosystem, prairie dogs in grasslands, or caribou on the northern tundra. Deep in a forest you may see a pine marten jump from tree to tree, or a banana slug may creep across your rainforest trail.

W is for Wildlife

Everyone likes to see wildlife.
Hey, look—there's a deer, there's a goose!
You might spy an owl or some tadpoles,
or maybe some elk or a moose!

Respect wildlife. Don't try to get close to or touch wildlife. Many wild animals may try to protect themselves if they feel threatened. Also, don't feed wildlife. Some foods are not good for animals, and feeding wildlife reduces the animal's natural fear of people, which can lead to bad human/wildlife encounters.

To see wildlife, you must be patient, observant, and quiet. If you're noisy, you'll scare animals away. However, in bear country noise is good—you don't want to startle a bear. Talk or sing as you hike, especially when going around bends or in thick brush.

Most hikers never see animals that can cause serious injury to humans. However, before you hike, you should find out if dangerous animals could be on your trail and what to do if you see them. If your trail goes through the habitat of large predators, such as bears or cougars, adults should carry pepper spray. If you see fresh prints or scat of these animals, leave the area immediately. And, if you encounter a dangerous animal, DON'T RUN—back away slowly. Running sets up an animal's instinct to chase and you can't outrun these animals.

A Trail to Travel: Whiteoak Canyon Falls Lower Trailhead in Shenandoah National Park has you walking past gigantic boulders and rock-hopping across creeks to a beautiful waterfall. (Virginia, 2.8 Miles, Easy–Moderate)

A compass tells you which direction you are going. The moving needle ALWAYS points north. When facing north, south is behind you, east is to your right, and west is to your left. Set your compass on your trail map, and line up north on the compass with north on the map to determine which direction your trail heads.

A Global Positioning System (GPS) device uses technology to track you as you hike and can lead you back to where you started. It's especially useful if you're *bushwhacking* (hiking off-trail). But beware! You may lose a signal, or your batteries might die, so bring a map and compass, too.

Orienteering is a fun competition using a compass and map to navigate an off-trail course ending at pre-placed checkpoint markers. The fastest one to complete the course is the winner.

A Trail to Travel: Explore the woodlands of Prince William Forest Park by following one of thirty orienteering courses. (Virginia, Ranging from 2–6 Miles, Easy–Moderate)

X

X

X is for X Marks the Spot

X marks a spot to navigate to,
but you must choose which way to head.
Is that way north? Which way is south?
Should we go east or west instead?

Yy

Y is for Year-Round Hiking

You can go hiking all year long;
you don't have to stay at home.
Even though it's wintertime,
your hiking feet can roam!

Many of America's state parks have First Day Hike events to start off the New Year. But what if it's snowy? That's okay—you'll see the world in a different way when you hit the trail in the snow.

A frozen world is beautiful! Snow crystals sparkle like diamonds, waterfalls become ice sculptures, and there's a peaceful quietness. But wait . . . Do you see animal tracks? What else is enjoying this winter wonderland?

Dress in layers and choose footwear that will keep your feet dry. Don't forget sunglasses—it's bright in the snow. Trekking poles will help keep you from slipping, and remember when choosing your trail, hiking in the snow is slower.

It's easy to hike in a few inches of snow, but if the snow is deep, try snowshoeing. It's another fun way to hike in winter.

A Trail to Travel: Yosemite National Park's Tuolumne Grove of Giant Sequoias Trail makes a great snow hike. (California, 2.5 Miles, Easy–Moderate)

Z is for Zest and Zeal

When you hike with zest and zeal,
you'll find that it is true:
the more you hike, the better you'll feel
'cause hiking is good for you!

Hiking is good for your body! You get a whole-body workout, strengthening your muscles, bones, heart, and lungs. Natural sunshine produces vitamin D in your body, giving you a strong immune system, which helps keep you from getting sick.

Hiking is good for your mind! Worried about something, or in a bad mood? Studies show hiking reduces stress and anxiety, and that the sounds of nature make you feel happier. Hiking also increases your attention span, helps you focus, and gets creative juices flowing.

Hiking is good for friends and family! It's a great way to connect with each other.

Hiking is good for the world! When hiking, you learn about nature, leading you to become more environmentally aware and responsible.

A Trail to Travel: Zion National Park's Emerald Pools Trail winds below canyon walls to three desert oases and a waterfall. (Utah, 2.2 Miles, Easy–Moderate)

Learn the Parts of a Compass

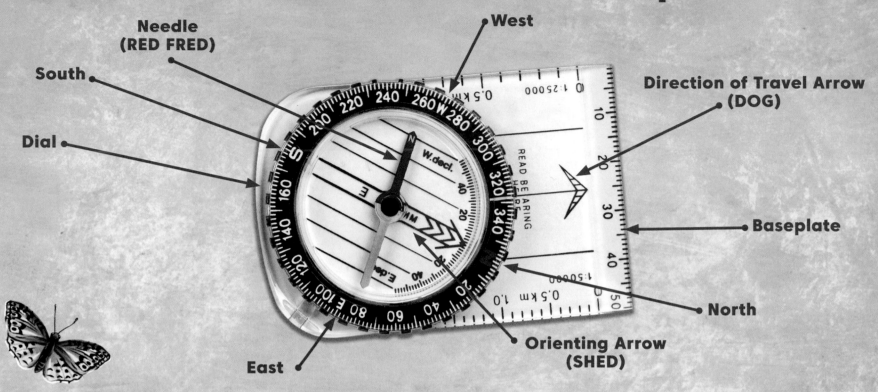

The Dial: The circle is the dial. It has letters—N, E, S, and W—representing the four different cardinal directions: north, east, south, and west. It also has numbers, telling different *degrees*, which is how to describe the direction if you are going at an angle between two cardinal directions. The numbers go from 0° to 360°, making a complete circle, starting and ending at north.

The Needle: In the middle of the dial is a moving needle. Let's call it RED FRED because the part you focus on is usually red. RED FRED **ALWAYS** points north, no matter how the dial around it is turned.

The Orienting Arrow: Inside the dial is the orienting arrow. Let's call it the SHED because it kind of looks like a tall building with a pointy roof. The SHED always points to the letter *N*. When you turn the dial, the shed turns with it.

The Direction of Travel Arrow: On the baseplate is the direction of travel arrow. We'll call it the DOG, which stands for **D**irection **O**f **G**o. You point the DOG the direction you want to go.

How Do You Use A Compass?
Put **RED FRED** in the **SHED** and Follow the **DOG**!
You'll need a baseplate compass to practice.

Let's try going due (or directly) east.

1. Turn the dial until the letter *E* lines up with the DOG.

2. Hold the compass flat and level. Keep your elbows close to your sides and have the compass stick out flat in front of your belly button. The DOG should point straight away from you, parallel with the ground, not at the sky.

3. Put RED FRED in the SHED by moving your feet to turn your whole body—not by twisting your body or moving the compass.

4. Look to see where the DOG is pointing. Does it point toward a rock, a tree, or some other object in the distance? That object is your *sighting*.

5. Keeping RED FRED in the SHED, go where the DOG points by heading toward your sighting. You're now going east!

6. Try going west, south, and north, too. Just line up a directional letter with the DOG, turn your body to put RED FRED in the SHED, then take a sighting and head toward it.

What if directions say to go a certain number of degrees? Do the same as above, but instead of using a directional letter, use the degree number. Let's practice with 220°.

1. Turn the dial until 220 lines up with the DOG.

2. Move your body until RED FRED is in the SHED, take a sighting, and start walking toward it.

Try the following activity and see where you end up!

1. Place a penny at your feet. Turn the compass dial to 60 and put RED FRED in the SHED.

2. Keeping RED FRED in the SHED, take 20 steps. (Make all your steps the same size.)

3. Turn the dial to south. Put RED FRED in the SHED and go 20 more same-sized steps.

4. Turn the dial to 300. Put RED FRED in the SHED and go 20 more steps.

5. Where did you end up? Did you come back to the penny? If not, try again. Remember: make your steps all the same size and keep RED FRED in the SHED while you walk.

For Tucker and Anna—
May the trails you travel lead you on a lifetime of adventures.
Love, Grandma

♥

For Zade, Fadwa, Windsor, and Jon Crewe

—Sharisse

Text Copyright © 2024 Judy Young
Illustration Copyright © 2024 Sharisse Steber
Design Copyright © 2024 Sleeping Bear Press

SLEEPING BEAR PRESS™
2395 South Huron Parkway, Suite 200
Ann Arbor, MI 48104
www.sleepingbearpress.com

Printed and bound in the United States.

10 9 8 7 6 5 4 3 2 1

Library of Congress Cataloging-in-Publication Data

Names: Young, Judy, 1956- author. | Steber, Sharisse, illustrator.
Title: T is for trails : a hiking alphabet / written by Judy Young
and illustrated by Sharisse Steber.
Description: Ann Arbor, MI : Sleeping Bear Press, 2024. | Audience: Ages 6-10 |
Summary: "Poetry and expository text give readers an A-to-Z guide on how to prepare
for outdoor hiking adventures. Topics include information on gear, clothing, and
safety rules, along with recommended trails to travel. Front and back matter includes
information on trail symbols and instructions on how to read a compass"
— Provided by publisher.
Identifiers: LCCN 2023033429 | ISBN 9781534112773 (hardcover)
Subjects: LCSH: Hiking—Juvenile literature. | Alphabet books.
Classification: LCC GV199.52 .Y68 2024 | DDC 796.51—dc23/eng/20230719
LC record available at https://lccn.loc.gov/2023033429

Photo credit: © RG-vc/Shutterstock, page 38